Rethinking Corporate Sustainability -
If Only We Ran the Planet Like a Shop!
Positive Thoughts to Help Make Sustainable Development Happen in Business

Alan Knight, PhD, OBE

© *future*THINK Press 2012

Alan Knight, PhD, OBE

Rethinking Corporate Sustainability - If Only We Ran the Planet Like a Shop! Positive Thoughts to Help Make Sustainable Development Happen in Business

ISBN: 978-1-105-70041-5

If you are interested in these ideas, please visit www.dralanknight.com

Contents

The dream is a world where every company, every organisation in the world answers this question:

My product's positive and negative contribution towards helping the world achieve 9 billion sustainable lifestyles by 2050 are...

This pamphlet explains the thinking behind such a dream.

About me: Alan Knight, PhD, OBE

I graduated as a geologist and marine biologist in the late 80s, but soon found that counting dead, muddy marine worms was not what I was born to do. I took a leap of faith and entered the retail world, having guessed (correctly, as it turned out) that the eco-thing would one day touch shopping, and that (somehow) a geologically trained dead worm counter could help shops face up to the eco-challenge. After a few months in the London toyshop, Hamleys, my lucky break was being invited to join the UK home improvement retailer B&Q as its first environment manager. This was the first of several such roles for me in UK retail. It took me around the world and led to my involvement in the creation of the Forest Stewardship Council, shaping government policy on eco-labeling and the numerous visits and opportunities to change how links in supply chains of everyday products bring products to the market.

At Kingfisher, B&Q's parent company, I helped coordinate social and environmental policies for all companies owned by Kingfisher worldwide. From there, I moved to the global brewer, SABMiller, where I produced their first group-wide sustainable development plan, including a group-wide governance system.

In 2006, I founded my own company, Single Planet Living, through which I helped businesses large and small develop their own sustainable development strategies. After 5 years, I joined Business in the Community as their Environmental Sustainability Director.

In 2010, I helped launch the Global Association for Corporate Sustainability Officers (GACSO) after a group of my peers recognized that sustainability needed more resonance with businesses, and the need to codify and nurture the career of the fulltime sustainability professional (www.gacso.org).

I continue to teach on the Cambridge Programme for Sustainability Leadership and I am a visiting professor at Exeter University Business School. I have sat on or chaired several think tanks including the Advisory Committee for Consumer Products and the Environment (ACCPE), which unpicked the failure of a single pan-European eco-labeling scheme and suggested the replication of the white goods energy labels for cars and buildings. Whilst sitting on the Sustainable Development Commission, I introduced the concept of 'choice editing' and 'product road-mapping'.

This twenty year journey has helped me shape a can-do, positive narrative on sustainable development. This narrative might come across as simplistic, but it is well informed through real life experiences and contrasts. It draws on the combined emotional and technical intelligence developed by being confronted with; a child making brass door handles in squalor in India; the memory of another child's face when the toy they dreamed for was out of stock; the sight of a beautifully laid-out garden centre ready for the Easter rush; the destruction of a tropical forest that supplied the timber for the garden benches or seeing an over-weight child enjoying a second burger for lunch in the UK.

It might not be strong on academic references, but it does not need to be: its purpose is to build first-hand experiences through humour, metaphors, and clarity to help business leaders and others value and embrace the sustainability challenge.

Here are 9 of my positive thoughts on the matter. I hope you enjoy them.

Alan Knight, PhD, OBE

E-mail - Alan@Dralanknight.com

www.dralanknight.com

Positive Thought One: Sustainability Will happen

One obvious but rarely stated positive thought is that sustainability is inevitable. Why? Because unsustainability is unsustainable - the clue is in the word. Unsustainability is, by definition, the state of affairs before sustainability arrives. As such it cannot last forever. To do so, it would have to be sustainable!

Would you agree that a growth based economy requiring 3 planets worth of natural resources to supply the 7 billion population locks too many people into poverty? That those who have access to modern lives suffering from obesity and diabetes while failing to achieve satisfaction is unsustainable? If so, you agree that something will change.

We cannot choose unsustainability from sustainability. The only choice we have is the nature of the sustainable outcome: Do we want one that favours modern living and commerce, or one that hinders it?

There are three extreme possible sustainable outcomes:

- Nature-led sustainability – nature takes control, eco-system collapses, and disease culls mankind to balance our population with other species. Nature has done this throughout the fossil record and could well do so again. Why should the human species be safe from virtual or actual extinction?

- Human-nature led sustainability - the darker elements of human greed, denial, and conflict lead us to ignore the opportunity of global collaboration. Instead, we seek to protect what is ours. Tensions become conflicts, and conflicts become wars: water wars, climate change migration leading to wars, and so on. As a consequence, human populations and the quality of their lives decline to levels where such tensions are elevated, either through victory or negotiation.

- Human intellect-led sustainability - we seek the right balance between nature and our appetite for modern lifestyles (aka 'civilisation'). This is the positive outcome to which the sustainability agenda is driving.

The claim that famine, natural disaster, and war are one path to sustainability is at one level true, since they take out an excess of people and consumption, and manage growth by default. But it is not an outcome that serves mankind well, which is why an outcome based on the lives we want (using the best of human intellect, spirit and creativity) must be the right outcome for sustainability. The challenge is that we have to do many things differently: unlike with the other two approaches to sustainability, where we only need to wait, then complain.

These extremes are deliberately crude. I wanted to make the point that, with 9 billion people on the way by 2050, and with most enjoying or wanting to enjoy the modern, comfortable, 'Plasma TV' lifestyle that many in the west do, we should deploy the best available intellect to make sustainability the tool by which that lifestyle is available for all of the 9 billion, and for every generation that follows.

In reality, natural disasters, war, and innovation will always occur at the same time, but the key question sustainable development raises is: just how much effort or inventions do we want to make now so that society can shape sustainable outcomes for the future? How do we develop 'civilisations' which are resilient to unavoidable disaster? What civil processes should we create to develop the right interventions and drive the right changes, rather than always just reacting to famine, war and natural disaster?

Current forecasts from the United Nations are for the global population to reach nine billion (9.15 billion) by 2050, rising to as much as fifteen billion by 2100.

We have to believe in the potential of civilisation to develop the technological and policy advances which allow business, governments, and the general public to make and deliver the right interventions. These interventions will be aimed at; much lower levels of poverty; more efficient use of natural resources; reduced pollution, improved levels of wellbeing; and at mitigating and slowing the impacts of climate change.

Halloween is a good example of what can be seen as the paradox of modern lives. Up until the 1990s, Halloween was just a fun evening; turning scrap clothes and empty boxes into a costumes and props. Combine that scrap with quality family time, and you end up with an innocent, cheap, and magical evening.

Now, in October, shops bulge with orange and plastic Halloween merchandise, which by definition, will only be used for a few dark hours on October 31st.

In 2011, Halloween day was marked by extensive news coverage of the birth of a child somewhere meant that there were at that moment seven billion humans living on the planet - a number which would continue to grow and grow. The second story on the UK BBC news was freak weather in New York. Many had already made the connection between the population and climate change, whilst many news programmes made reference to the children and Halloween the link between Halloween fancy dress and climate change was naturally not made, but there is a link.

Seven billion people wanting plastic Halloween hats and costumes and sweets will lead to more plastic being used and more being thrown away. Yes, it *is* that simple. The obvious solution is to say, "Don't provide plastic based Halloween hats and outfits.", and change expectations with respect to candy, sweets and treats.

But behind plastic based Halloween hats and costumes are jobs; people working in factories making hats and costumes for the lifestyle we currently enjoy. So how do we square this circle of lifestyle choices and moving people out of poverty through manufacturing, employment and consumption?

Poverty is cruel, and eradicating poverty requires commerce and trade – business ends poverty. At the moment, business includes coffee, tea, flowers, sweets and candies, mobile phones, plasma TVs, and plastic goods.

While it is easy for me to challenge the 2011 'plastic Halloween', somebody somewhere saw the business opportunity, unleashed their creative and entrepreneurial spirit, and brought products to market that people would buy; creating jobs and income for thousands. This is why 'trade, not aid' is the most successful approach to poverty reduction.

But eradicating poverty through 'trade not aid' has significant consequences for sustainability. The key challenge is, for now at least, that the numbers don't add up. To give seven billion people a 'plasma TV' lifestyle today would require three planets' worth of natural resources.

Wal-Mart would not run a promotion on say shorts if they knew that the demand would outstrip supply by three fold. The desire and need to see more people enjoy a better life is doing the same, we are creating demand for something we cannot supply.

What this (admittedly speculative) example suggests is simple: we need to rethink our supply arrangements to enable sustainability.

Notice something about this type of narrative: that there are no ethics in it thus far. People talk about the issue being driven by ethics, morals and values. Ending poverty, it can be argued, is a morals- and values- driven imperative. But it is also a major commercial challenge and opportunity. This is where we can begin to develop parallels with retailers, and speak of the planet as being like a shop. Retailers would never intentionally set up a proposition to their customers on which they could not deliver. But, in our 'planet as a shop' analogy, this is precisely what we are doing.

The challenge we have is simple: there isn't enough 'stuff' in existence to give everybody the lifestyle they are seeking. Our real challenge, then, is about preserving the lifestyle currently enjoyed in the developed world, while finding the mechanisms to make it available to more people.

Shops and modern 'plasma TV' lifestyles are not just a Western phenomenon – go to China, India, the Middle East and see shopping malls, local stores, and streets full of stalls, markets and shops. The desire for modern lifestyles crosses cultures, religions, and wealth brackets - as is evident everywhere. Shopping creates lifestyles people prefer, and millions of jobs in the supply chain to enable others to afford that lifestyle. I am not saying that this lifestyle is free from problems; what I am saying is that we need to acknowledge the buying and shopping trends around the world, and be positive because they may be the key to unlocking the challenges of sustainability.

Many environmental campaigners worry about the link between shopping and over consumption. They are, at one level, dead right. But you can see this challenge another way and think,

- "Aren't we clever, as human beings, that we can build the world's tallest building and shopping malls in a desert like Dubai?"
- "Aren't we clever? Isn't the plasma T.V. lifestyle clever?"
- "Aren't human beings clever, that they can invent that lifestyle?"

Over 9,000 years of human spirit and innovation have taken us from flint axes to plasma TVs. What a clever, adaptable people we are. What will we create next, what should we create next and why don't we?

My question is simple: can we apply some of that cleverness and an ability to adopt, adapt, and innovate to some of the challenges facing the world today? What appears to be wrong with the Dubai situation is that the tall building, the Burj Khalifa, is a wonderfully correct answer to the wrong exam question.

Rather than ask "what can we do to make us distinctive?", or, "how can we create an air conditioned shopping mall in a desert and make money from it?", we might have been better asking the question: "how do we create and develop a low-carbon city, and apply technology developed to make the world's tallest sustainable building functional to actually create a Green Energy centre?"

By getting the right answer to the wrong question, the Burj Khalifa is a symbol of our ingenuity and creativity failing to focus on what matters most and, consequently, our ingenuity and imagination being underused.

Mankind can at times be cruel and greedy, but these bad habits are not a function of modern lifestyles. They are rooted in something deeper and long lasting. Let us hope that we have consigned many of the worst atrocities to history: the pharaoh's pyramids were perhaps a bit greedy; the slaves and gladiators of Roman times would have struggled to get through today's humans rights laws; and the English habit of burning witches was perhaps an overreaction! So, let's not link today's human cruelty with modern lifestyles: cruelty is something that lies much deeper in our psychology.

Encouraging guilt and finding blame among those who aspire to modern day lifestyles fails to acknowledge that they are the result of inner human nature and technical genius. More importantly, the income generated by those lifestyles ultimately creates the educational opportunities and technological and scientific innovations that will finally lift the world from poverty.

So the good news is sustainability can happen and I believe we have the skills to create the sustainable outcome most people want. I offer this as my first of nine positive thoughts on sustainability. Success, however, needs the emergence of a positive, guilt-free and practical tone of voice and that is my second positive thought.

Positive Thought Two: Celebrate Modern Lifestyles

It is time that the environmental narrative acknowledged that most people want access to the modern, plasma TV lifestyle many have access to in emerging economies such as Brazil, Russia, India, Indonesia, and China.

Please do not take this metaphor literally. I mean that, on balance, people would prefer a lifestyle with access to modern communications, clean water, a comfortable home, reliable and safe travel, modern medicine, and quality education. The spirit, if not the reality, of what I am calling the "plasma TV lifestyle" is here to stay. What needs to happen, now and over the next 40 years, is the continued improvement of access for people to the lifestyles they want. Those lifestyles must also be made robust and resilient, both in terms of community and the planet, despite the pressure of population growth. I choose to believe that in the next 40 years, we can use all our intellectual and commercial abilities and power to deliver modern lifestyles for the whole of civilisation.

Daily life will, of course, be different. You need only look back over the past 40 years to see how lifestyles have changed. While the technology will be different, many aspects of family life will remain more or less the same.

Modern lifestyles as symbolised by the plasma TV are enabled by innovation and the logistical abilities of global commerce and public policy. However, in some countries, war and natural disasters make these lifestyles inaccessible.

In my travels around the world, I've visited most continents, and one of the most obvious observations is the huge contrast between lifestyles in, say, Papua New Guinea, to the plasma TV lifestyle I personally enjoy in the UK. In Papua New Guinea, local people depend on their forests for food, building materials, and cash. In many aspects, they have a sustainable lifestyle, in that they are few people, and they are not using much of the available 'stuff' available within a huge forest. They, however, do not see their lives and their forest quite like that. To make their lives easier, they would prefer more access to the modern things we enjoy, like medicine, education, clean water and electricity.

There is a link – some of the commercial sectors that supply the 'bits' of our modern lifestyle look to the forests of Papua New Guinea for their raw materials. The forest village leaders are continually pressured by foreign companies for their logs, land, and now their carbon credits. To protect their own destiny and their own resources, forest village leaders need viable alternatives to the seduction of the foreign loggers in neighbouring villages, and they need to understand the complexities of carbon trading. They need legal advice, they need infrastructure, and they need to be wise to the external world. To be safe from the consuming cash world, they need cash and communication. *Then the only way they can protect themselves from commerce is to be become part of it.*

Eradicating poverty is, therefore, commercially, politically, and morally desirable, and key to sustainability. The irony is that less poverty equates to more consumption.

I argue, however, that it's not the plasma TVs in themselves that are wrong, it's how the raw materials are harvested, the conditions in which they are made, and how they are disposed which causes the problem. The plasma TV outcome in *not* the problem – it's the clumsy nature of the inputs: it is 'how we do it' that is wrong, as opposed to 'it' being a bad thing.

The challenge is not our lifestyle, but the supply chains that contribute to it.

We can feel positive and proud of our modern lifestyle. What we need to reflect upon and change is how that lifestyle is provided.

Positive Thought Three: More Inspiration and Action, Less Guilt and Blame

I believe by 2052, our modern plasma TV lifestyles will be sustainable. If you challenge me, are you inadvertently giving everyone permission to try less, and even fail?

Rather than blaming individuals, public officials, and commerce for creating *un*sustainability, our energies are better served by supporting and inspiring leaders to focus their talents on re-engineering to provide more modern lifestyles using less "stuff". When we think of sustainable development, we should ask: What's the narrative?

Let's face it – mankind is very clever. The world's tallest building was built in the former deserts of Dubai. Is that a sign of man's ability to deliver complex projects – or a high-carbon folly? For me, the Burj Khalifa demonstrates us putting our minds to a challenge. We are good at taking on big challenges, so by seeing sustainable development as a challenge or project, we are more likely to deliver the changes we seek.

Environmentalists and business people are both horrified by the allegation that it takes 11,000 litres of water to make one beef quarter ponder, or 20,000 litres to make one kilo of coffee. But in that very waste lays an opportunity.

In business, we speak of 'agile' or 'lean' manufacturing – producing a product (like a quarter pounder) as efficiently and effectively as possible. If it really does take 11,000 litres of water, there is ample room for water savings in our burger supply chain. Sustainable development is applying that logic to every aspect of the modern plasma TV lifestyle. Using this approach, the 9 billion modern lives required by 2052 become more realistic.

The way we approach people and organisations who might be involved in something unsustainable really matters. The natural approach is to go in hard, criticise and humiliate. Traditional campaigns have worked to some extent, but look how sport coaches handle challenges. Imagine you are the coach of a children's sports team. You know (and you know the children know) that the opponents they are facing are much better; beating them is unlikely. The kids are in their team jersey and they are about to play. Which pep talk from you is likely to give them that extra bit of energy: one which focuses on their strengths, or one that reminds them how rubbish they are? It is a simple metaphor, but one which I wonder if the environmentalism movement could draw some lessons from. Which is more likely to be heard and followed: a technically correct pessimist, or a slightly inaccurate optimist?

Positive Thought Four: Embrace Your Best Business Skills to Achieve Sustainability

Hamleys, the big toy shop in London where I worked for 6 months, was a personal revelation. Their "can do, get it done" business attitude, especially getting the job done as best you can on that day rather than an endless search for perfection was a refreshing change from the methodical, evidence-centric world of science I had been living in.

My role at Hamleys was overseeing the telephone, mail orders, and shipments. Combining toys, Christmas, and shopping is a great formula to learn about people and getting things done. I learned more about people through the selling of teddy bears and jigsaw puzzles than I did in six years as an academic studying marine worms, geological strata, and other workings of the undersea environment.

The relationship and tension between peer-reviewed scientific academia, and the results focus of retail provided me with a solid foundation to combine the best of both in corporate sustainability. The academics seek out and try to understand complexity. Businesspeople just work from what they want, seeking a particular result. Sustainability has plenty of the former, but not enough of the latter. I think sustainability, therefore, has a lot to learn from shop-keeping or in fairness and business.

Some will find my idea of giving credit to good shop-keeping as a model for sustainability annoying because, at one level at least, it is shopping-related consumption that is seen by many to be the root of unsustainability. Shops encourage the desire for 'stuff', and generally rely on the exploitation of natural resources to make it. I do not deny those negatives, but I'm referring here to the attitude and skills that shop keepers have developed to manage supply, delivery, and customer focus which I believe could be better applied to our planet-scale problems.

To many, shop-keeping and retail add up to nothing more than, "stock it, sell it, and enjoy the profit". It is, however, quite the opposite and very complex. Hidden from the customer is the complexity of inventory management, logistics, oversea sourcing and high finance The apparent simplicity of a store is what makes it compelling to the customer. The clearer and more inspired the retail format, the more successful it is. What a lesson for sustainability!

Let us now look at 'sustainable development'. To many, it is the balance of environmental, social, and economic issues. This is correct – but balance is not a call for action.

What does that balance look like in the 'shop window' of sustainability? It is unclear what it is people are being asked to do. If only we could make sustainability more action-focused.

Instead of selling sustainability as 'balance', why not say instead that it is, "a way we can feed, house and support all the people who live on the planet, without destroying that planet!"? That, now, is something people could be persuaded to 'buy'.

Could it be that simple a proposition? That is why the shop keeping metaphor is compelling – shop keeping provides us with the stuff of life, and so does sustainable development. Good retailers nurture their supply chains, bad ones harm them.

So if the shop-keeping model can bring some good, can it bring *more* good? What if a shop keeper was asked to run the biggest shopping challenge facing mankind: creating the right supply chains to feed, clothe and enable contentment for the billions of people who will inhabit the planet in the future?

I believe it is time to strip ethics and judgement from business and make it practicable by posing the ultimate challenge through the language of retail. If a group of people had to run the planet and help resolve the current issues of poverty, over consumption, pollution and declining life satisfaction, which group has the best skills to achieve this; scientists, or business people like shop keepers?

Naturally, the answer falls at some mid-point where everyone has a contribution. I suspect, however, that most gurus underestimate the potential contribution of shop-keepers and other business leaders. I will build the case that business people have a lot to offer by asking one simple question: What if shop keepers were asked to resolve the planet challenges of consumption, climate change, poverty and declining wellbeing? In other words…

What if retailers were asked to run the planet?

Imagine yourself as the Managing Director of Wal-Mart or the CEO of *Save-on-Foods* or TESCO or President of *Home Depot*. You can get drills, saws, and lumber from around the world. You can source Halloween costumes from China. You can meet timelines, make money, create lots of jobs, and give customers what they want. How would you apply this knowledge and skill-set for the whole planet – the ultimate shop? We'll be out of stock on some key items – water in some places, food supplies, raw materials, and uranium to run our MRI machines, for example - soon. Can you do something about this, please?

A good retail CEO would pull together his leadership team and advisors and develop a focused brainstorm.

These always start with a proposition (remember, we are running the planet as a shop and a business). I think the proposition, or mission, she would suggest would be something like:

"We will provide: food, shelter, homes, and wellbeing for people everywhere, forever"

So the next stage of a sound business activity is to start looking at the numbers – the basics, like customer count and volume demand.

Mankind appeared 160,000 years ago. There was steady organic growth in customer count through the 160 millennia until the mid 18th century, when population started to grow dramatically from a few 100 million, to the first billion by the turn of the nineteenth century, two billion by the 1930s, and 7 billion on Halloween day in 2011. The forecast is for 9 billion persons by 2050.

160 millennia is a lot of years to comprehend. If we condensed the 160,000 years down to just 30 years – the average life of most companies – the scale of the ask becomes clearer. Squeezing that 160,000 years into 3 equates to a growth of 3,000% in customer count in the last quarter of those 30 years. Name one business that delivered such growth in its 30th year!

The amount each customer buys is known as "volume"or, in retail speak, "sales per transaction", or even "basket value". At the dawn of civilisation (ignoring the odd Pharaoh), the ask of the planet from each customer was a few logs for kayaks, fish for food, and iron ore for weapons. Three hundred years ago, sales per basket was still low– there were tall hats for some, leather leggings and carts and horses, there were some cooking items, and a lot of vegetables and fish. Quite a small number of transactions per customer back then, but by 2012, they are buying the plasma TV lifestyle. So we have larger volumes, growing very fast, with higher turnover of goods and higher value sales producing higher potential profits. We are increasing the customer count and volume simultaneously.

An exciting new customer base, but scary in terms of our ability to deliver products. The challenge for us is making sure the supply chain is right.

Sustainability is a supply chain challenge – 9 billion modern lifestyles by 2050.

Are our supply chains capable of delivering all of this? According to the World Wild Fund for Nature (UK) Living Planet Report, published in 2002, the global average consumption of natural resources (what's known as our *ecological footprint*) is 2.3 hectares of natural resources per person, per year. In the developed countries of the Western world, this figure rises to around 5 hectares. As a result, the WWF states: *"if everyone around the world consumed natural resources at the rate that we currently do in the UK, we would need three planets to support us."*

No retailer could sustain sales of an item if the supply base could not replenish the inventory at the same rate of sales. That is very basic retail.

Are we looking after the supply chains? There are some sixty or more products produced from forested lands, ranging from textiles, to pharmaceuticals, to wood for framing houses, to bio-fuels for fuelling aircraft, cars and trucks. But they also supply mankind with soul and spirit. We like to walk in them, to see animals graze in them; we see them as a place which birds can be safe, and as places that can sequester carbon. We ask a lot of forests, and a retailer skilled in supply chain management would nurture the assets they provide.

It would do this through audits and pricing. Most retailers audit their factories to ensure that they have the operating standards to meet quality and volume projections. If Wal-Mart used its audit methods to audit the entire world's forest estates ability (under the current management regime) to provide all the desired needs in 2050, would the global forest estate pass or fail?

Do we value nature in our supply chain enough? How should the global supply chain value a bee? Bees provide pollination for free – so they are a good low-cost part of our supply chain. Imagine if we had to replace the bee with people or a machine. In China, they are – they are paying people to do the work of the bees they have lost.

Imagine this: you are going into a major supermarket tomorrow and you've heard they've got this really crazy promotion on – everything in aisles 1-15, you pay for normally, but in aisles 16-20, everything's going to be free. Just take as much as you want. What will that store look like in the first hour of the shopping experience? Then think about the images you often see of the Amazon rainforest. Because we don't place a realistic value on what nature is able to provide for us, we have a major challenge with our rainforests. By placing a value on forested lands for all of the 'services' it provides (which are known as ecosystem services) we can best assess how to price access to forested lands. Retailers are already good at getting the price right – we can learn.

Let's go back to the proposition – the delivery of wellbeing.

People are getting heavier. Almost one in four adults in Britain is classed as obese. This figure could rise to eight out of 10 men and seven out of 10 women by 2020, according to recent reports. A new Statistics Canada study suggests one in four Canadian adults is clinically obese, compared with one in three in the United States. Among men in both Canada and the U.S., the increase was highest among those aged 60 to 74, while in women, obesity increased the most among those aged 20 to 39. So perhaps, despite the great products we provide people for the modern lifestyle, we need to help reverse some habits to help people look after their health. If not, the retail value proposition will not be delivered.

Retail brands are made or broken on the delivery of customer satisfaction. In our metaphor, customer satisfaction equates to life satisfaction, or happiness. Some governments have started to measure life satisfaction of its citizens and the message is not good.

Despite considerable economic growth over the last fifty years around the world, people are no happier now than they were shortly after Truman came to power in the United States, as the graph below shows. Happiness remains largely flat as per capita GDP grows exponentially.

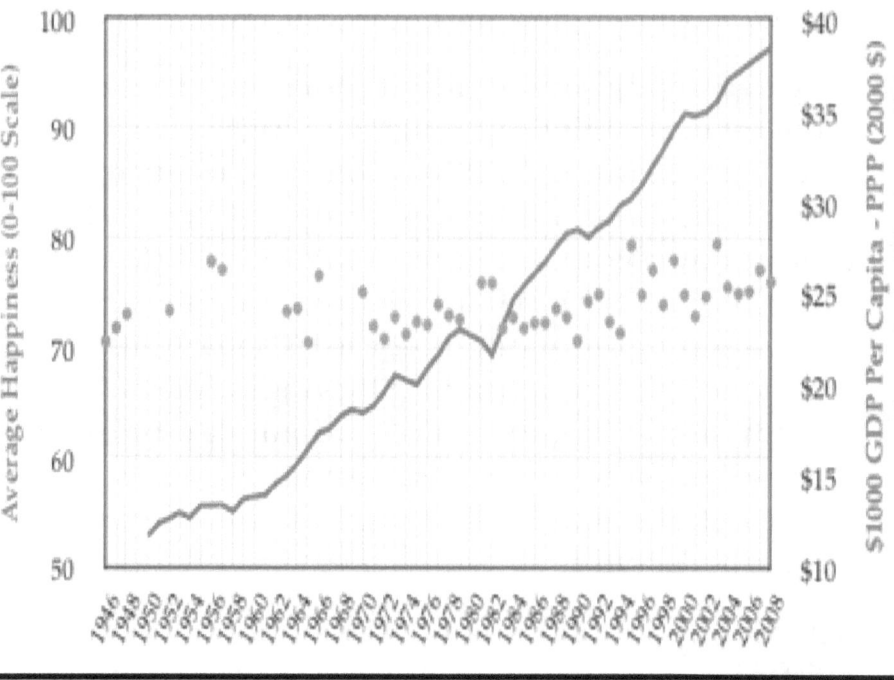

Figure 1: Happiness (Dots) vs. GDP Growth (Solid Line)

In summary – our imaginary retailer (let's call it Planet Earth Retail Chain) needs a turnaround strategy related to these key points:

1. Massive and rapid growth in customer numbers
2. Massive growth in transaction value per customer
3. Pending 'out of stocks'
4. Declining quality of supply base
5. Poor cost and pricing
6. Inconsistent delivery of the wellbeing proposition
7. Declining customer satisfaction

These are the seven symptoms, any one of which can cause the downfall of our retail chain. Many businesses have uncovered such trends in their backyards, reversed them, and have since flourished. Can we do this for Planet Earth Retail Chain?

Staying with this analogy of the planet as a shop, sustainable development requires us to run the planet with the same rigorous discipline as we manage a successful shop! I sometimes laugh when companies ask me, "What is the business case for sustainability?" I suggest to them:

You invented it. It's discipline. It's governance. It's managing your growth in a way that enables you to deliver it. Basically, businesses have failed because they haven't followed the principles you were taught in your business schools, and by your experiences.

Sustainable development is no different. It requires us to apply the principles of sound global retail business to managing the planet and the supply chains to feed, house, and clothe 9 billion people.

This analogy works for other sectors: Would a financial institution bankroll planet earth? Would an insurance company underwrite it?

Different companies can apply their own contexts to the planet-scale challenge, and the result would be the same. Business discipline applied at a planet level could deliver a lot of what sustainability requires. At its most basic, any company can multiply its average transaction by the 9 billion they might one day be expected to process, and data will reveal the challenge within their own sector. If their sector cannot not even service 9 billion, what hope is there for all the other sectors? The answers lie in a can–do approach, innovation, and the re-engineering of supply chains.

Positive Thought Five: Treat Sustainability as a Supply Chain Project

This pamphlet opened with the notion that *"You can't be unsustainable forever"*.

Whether you are a business leader or an environmentalist, by agreeing that the current way we supply lifestyles is unsustainable, you are also agreeing that something is going to change. Unsustainability, after all, is the state of affairs that exists before sustainability. All we can choose is which version of sustainable outcome we end up with; the likelihood of achieving the outcome we prefer depends on the timing and degree of intervention we make.

 I have already listed the extremes of sustainable outcomes:

- Nature-led sustainability, or 'extinction'
- Human-nature led sustainability, or 'war'
- Human intellect-led sustainability or 'civilisation'

Extinction and war have nothing but dreadful political and commercial value, meaning the outcome we want is civilization. We *could* put our modern lives on hold and "go back to better times". Some environmental commentators romanticise and celebrate a country-living lifestyle as sustainable.

In 2010 the BBC in the UK aired a series called *It isn't Easy Being Green*. A middle aged husband moved his family into a derelict water mill, which they restored. They grew organic vegetables and made their own energy. I lived in London, and I checked the real estate pages. I could not find 20 million derelict watermills to house every UK household. If I could, I don't think it would be sustainable – 20 million households in the countryside would wreck the countryside.

A few low impact county lifestyles are fine, but not replicable for the entire population. Cities are more efficient at providing for high populations. This means a sustainable global economy will have a high proportion of the population living in cities. This re-enforces the notion that modern plasma TV lifestyles will be urban-centric. Once again, this brings sustainable development down to the basics – it's about making the modern plasma TV lifestyle available for 9 billion people by 2050, whilst improving the wellbeing and life satisfaction for all on the planet.

Typically, sustainable development is described as finding the balance between environmental and social issues, and economics. Intellectually, this is right and understandable, but where is the call to action? Balance implies: being careful; steadiness; slowing down; or even stopping. Paradoxically, to make sustainable development happen, urgency is needed; action and speed. We are running out of stock in our supply chain to deliver the lifestyle we want. People are still suffering from poverty, while others are suffering from excess. We urgently need to reengineer the supply chain to make the best 'bits' accessible to more, and eliminate the worst 'bits'.

We need to find new ways of making modern lives accessible so that they can be accessible for 9 billion people. The retail metaphor serves us well. The core principle of good retail buying is a clear specification for the product the buyer wants to stock. If sustainable development is about the procurement of 9 billion sustainable lifestyles, what would the buying specification of a sustainable lifestyle be?

Telling people how they ought to live their lives can be uncomfortable. People must have the freedom to decide how they want to live their lives, but I do not think it is unreasonable to suggest some framing principles about what issues matter to help make those lives more sustainable.

Sticking with a positive approach, let's imagine that society did deliver those 9 billion sustainable lifestyles by 2050. Only one planet's worth of natural resources; every country achieving its carbon targets; and problematic health trends (like obesity and depression) under control.

How would someone in that wonderful future describe the differences between their life and the lives we lead in the unsustainable world of today? I imagine they might list ten key differences:

1. *"I manage my own self esteem and health"* - Our bodies were designed for a hunter/ gatherer lifestyle, eating a specific menu of foods prepared in simple ways. We now have a more sedentary lifestyle; working at our desks, watching our TVs, eating more processed higher calorie foods, driving not walking. We have chosen to change how we use our bodies, and the fuel we use to drive our bodies.

Given this, it's no wonder our bodies are changing shape. In a sustainable society, we will be (on average) much better at maintaining our health. We will also understand how to manage a sense of self-worth and appreciation for life which help keep mental health problems at bay.

2 *"I live within financial limits - personally and at a national level"*. You cannot spend money you do not have and cannot afford to pay back if borrowed. It is about living within your limits. In a

sustainable world, this would be how everyone lives, but of course, in that world everyone will have enough to live on.

3. *"The products I buy help everyone in the supply chain achieve a better life"* If I want a rug in my house, the person who made it should also be better off for my buying it. So, in a sustainable world there will be no exploitation of child labour, nor will waterways be polluted by dyes and detergents. Everyone in that rug supply chain, from sheep farmer to loom operator to customer, will have their lifestyle enhanced by the rug transaction. There are many products that are successfully embedding social and environmental standards into their supply chain. For example:

- Rug Market – avoiding the exploitation of child labour in rugs
- Forest Stewardship Council - sustainable forest management for wood and paper
- Rainforest Alliance- many products, like tea and coffee
- Roundtable on Sustainable Palm Oil – palm oil
- Marine Stewardship Council – fish from the wild
- Marine Aquarium Council – aquarium fish
- Better Soya Initiative, Better Sugar Cane Initiative, Better Cotton Initiative – the names speak for themselves

It's a popular model, with over 60 product stewardship schemes and counting, and over 250 eco-labels. If you are the Sustainability Officer of a retailer the sheer number is a distraction. What an interesting success story.

4. *"I use clean and renewable energy "*– This means using less and finding cleaner, lower carbon ways of making it. Quite a lot has been said on this elsewhere!

5." *I am active in a vibrant community"* – One of the downsides of cities is that neighbourly spirit is less than in villages. Although we live very close to each other, we seem less neighbourly than those who live in villages or the country. Some weird psychology seems to be going on there. Maybe the cause is the pace of life, the cosmopolitan nature of it, but whatever the reason, societies that achieve sustainability will be more neighbourly, where people will automatically look after the infirm lady next door and not complain when the state cannot help. Who would argue against that?

6. *"I live in a high trust society in which I talk with, rather than at, people"* – This is where the environmental movement might need more focus. The over-preaching and criticisms of the very people they wish to change may be turning people off, creating more inertia and negative opinion, rather than unlocking the available talent and willingness to change. Many look at the Forest Stewardship Council (FSC) as an eco label to inform consumer choice. That's all correct, but what made the FSC ahead of its time was the degree and nature of its collaboration. The FSC standards were agreed upon by consensus across sectors who normally would have never met. As part of the FSC, the indigenous people of Peru may have sat at the same table as the lumber buyer for B&Q or Home Depot, and the tissue buyer for Kleenex may have worked alongside the forest manager for the World Wide Fund for Nature in Germany. With so many supply chains needing so much collaboration, such trust and conversation will become mainstream.

7. *"We balance technology with simplicity* – Look at the Prius motor car - a piece of technology which did not exist in the early 1990s. Whilst the Prius is an eco-friendly car, using it to drive a distance which you could easily walk is still an eco-unfriendly thing to do. A sustainable future would find this balance between simplicity (walking) and high technology (eco-cars). Who knows? By 2050, the meeting I drive to the station and catch the train to attend might not involve travel at all, since I will be talking via three dimensional video.

8. *"My leaders (political and business) have courage"*. Sustainability will not be achieved, or even maintained, by small incremental steps. Bold people will make bold decisions which, for most others, would have been too dangerous or scary. Remember the planet and shop metaphor: retailers in trouble are more likely to rescue themselves by bold actions, not incremental steps. The same may be true for achieving the 9 billion challenge.

9. *"Far less 'stuff' is used to provide my lifestyle"*. This point is very subtle. It does *not* say, "I will use far less stuff in my life", although we *will* probably use a bit less. But if it really does take 11,000 litres of water to make one beef burger, then most of the potential saving is in how the burger is made, not how the consumer uses it.

The conclusion I have reached after 20 years visiting many different links in the supply chains of the products we use in our lives is there is still huge amounts of inefficiency in the creation of the goods with which you live your lifestyle and because of that there are many more products we can obtain from what we have without causing further harm to nature.

10. *"The true value of nature is protected by economics"*. Nine billion sustainable lifestyles will only be achieved after we have

improved our appreciation and management of eco-services. One approach to this challenge is being explored in depth in a number of places; from Alberta to China and from the U.S. to India. It is known as "eco systems services" – seeing the forest as a provider of a natural resources which can be valued in monetary, social and ecological terms. The basic idea is that the attributes of a piece of forested land, such as Forests of Papua New Guinea or the forest around the Rocky Mountains in Alberta, are assessed for the value they offer to a society. These valuations, often monetary estimates, cover such things as: carbon sequestration, watershed impacts, biodiversity, contributions to manufacturing output, grazing, hunting, fishing, leisure and tourism, aesthetics, and other aspects of forested lands.

Just after Christmas in 2010, the UK government announced its intention to sell the whole of the UK public forest estate (200,000 hectares), including many royal forests, state-owned ancient woodlands, sites of special scientific interest, heartland, campsites, farms and sporting estates – all of which the government manages on our behalf. They wanted to transfer all of this from Crown ownership into private hands. What the government failed to realise (but were soon made to through a united campaign), was that the forest is much more than an economic resource. While the government saw privatization as a means of job and wealth creation, they forgot the range of uses for which forested lands are valued by communities. They didn't do the trade-off math required. They got it wrong and backed off reasonably quickly. Today, economics only look at ecosystems for the cash. In a world of 9 billion sustainable lifestyles, economics would value the softer benefits too.

Nine billion quality lifestyles is a big ask of the planet. At the moment we are harming people and the planet to provide for the 7 billion alive today with a high proportion having a life where the adjective "quality" would be impossible to use. In this narrative, sustainability is the tool that finds the capacity to deliver the other 2 billon while doing less harm. It *is* that simple, and must be a part of good commerce and sound politics. The list of ten above encompasses the key trends or issues where interventions are required to reach that 9 billion challenge. Some of these ten are easy, and some are harder to achieve; but none contradict any sensible ambition to improve our current quality of life or business models.

Positive Thought Six: Having a Product Story You are Proud Of

If your products could talk – what would they say?

It's Saturday night. You are slumped on the sofa watching TV, and the familiar theme music for your favourite chat show comes on. The host strolls down the stairs:

"Tonight, I will be talking to," he says, but this time it is not the usual roster of A and B list celebrities.

"Flown in from India, especially for us, a brass door knob. We have an organic strawberry from Sussex, England, and we have a garden bench from Vietnam".

This intrigues you because you are the supplier of one of those products.

What would these items talk about? Well, true to the host's style, they would talk about their life stories. Trust me: they would be just as interesting as Posh and Becks, or Elton John!

Brass Door Knob would describe childhood memories of being part of a pile of European scrap; perhaps from an old ship or old pub fittings. It would describe a sea crossing to India, where it was melted down and cast into door knobs. Castings would not be in a single factory, but in one of hundreds of small cottage units. The process was dangerous, involving hot molten metal and filthy smoke. There might even be a short video clip.

You can imagine the scene – an Indian Village, huts glowing from the light of the furnaces and sparks lighting up the night as molten brass is poured from crucibles to the sand moulds. Brass door knob would tell of its journey to the polishing units: dark basements where people sat in long rows, one person per polishing wheel. For thirty minutes or so, they pushed the knob against the polishing wheel until it was scratch free and shining. Polishing created a fine powder which filled the air, caked the walls, and covered the floor to a depth of several centimetres. The polishers were so filthy that all that could be seen was the white of their eyes. Some of the dust settled in their lungs, planting the seeds of tuberculosis. As for Door Knob's future, it had a sea crossing to the UK, and a few days or weeks on the shelves of your local hardware retailer before several happy years on the door of a house until it was retired and replaced by a new more trendy design. Who knows? It might be scrapped and sent back to India to start the whole journey all over again!

Organic strawberry has a far better story to tell. It probably had a caring, chemical-free rearing, and is excited at the prospect of telling the audience about the satisfied customer enjoying a healthy, nutritious dessert.

Garden bench could have a good or bad story. It may boast with pride its story of a high quality of forest management - so good, in fact, that it has the been certified by the Forest Stewardship Council and is now proudly being displayed in a retailer like John Lewis, Home Depot, or B&Q - retailers which proactively source FSC products. Alternatively, the story could be the older and far sadder story of rainforest destruction, wildlife murder, and the exploitation of forest people.

Every product we buy, eat, or use in our life has a story to tell. The compelling common sense of fair trade, 'one planet' living, or organic living would be so obvious to retailers and consumers that it would, I'm sure, be mainstream.

Many business people spend time (perhaps too much) on the conference circuit listening to human beings give their views on the role of business and consumers in creating a more sustainable future. Sometimes, it is mind numbingly painful to listen as people explain what needs to be done. Sometimes, I wonder if we are making the story too complicated.

All products – food, toilet seats, hammers and wallpaper – begin in the natural environment. All those same products have had some element of production, either in small cottage units or huge factories. This means thousands of peoples' lives are made better or more difficult by that production, and a large proportion of those products have travelled huge distances from the Far East or Eastern Europe, crossing borders and cultures. Wallpaper from Finland, pine shelves from South Africa, lights from China, lampshades from the Philippines, rugs from Turkey, coir mats from India and even flowers from Kenya. I bet you did not know your living room was really a multicultural society of objects!

So if you, as a business person, look at your offer and ask these questions...

1) Where in nature did the raw materials come from – a forest, a field, the sea?
2) In what country was this product made?
3) How many people were involved in making this product and what are their lives like?
4) What will happen to this product when I do not want it anymore?
5) And (as asked already) how much raw material would be required to make my product available to a world of 9 billion?

...in most cases, you will not know. Imagine if the products could just tell you. If the story were of environmental destruction and human rights violations, would you shuffle with embarrassment? Conversely, what if the story demonstrated environmental enhancement and a genuine case of improving peoples' lives? Would you be proud of that product? This argument works even better for the manufacturers and retailers who brought them to your door.

In my conference speeches I often ask: "If your products could talk, would you be proud or embarrassed about the story they told?" I then deliver an even more thought provoking challenge – do you even know what that story would be?

Knowing the story unlocks action. A lot can be done. As I said, my own career in corporate sustainability started at B&Q. The decision to create the position I was lucky enough to fill was prompted by a question from a journalist - "Where does your tropical wood come from?" The marketing director answered, "I don't know." The journalist's response was provocative – "If you do not know, you do not care!"

The situation in 1990 was that B&Q's products were made with wood from unknown sources and, without knowing the source, it was impossible to provide any reassurance on quality of forest management. I toured the major forest sources and compiled data. We knew enough then to take action. In 2011, B&Q announced that all of its wood based products came from known forests, certified as being managed to a set of 3rd party environmental and social standards from either the Forest Stewardship Council (which B&Q helped create) or from the PEFC, which was created as an alternative choice to the FSC.

This announcement took 20 years of supply chain re-engineering to achieve. But they did it. I was lucky enough to kick start the process but it was a long, hard, slog for many people across the business, and 100s of supply chains impacted.

Knowing the product story is a start. With that knowledge, you can eliminate the obvious bad things – but how does it relate to the bigger 9 billion challenge? What now needs to done to ensure that your product offering is having either a neutral or positive contribution to making 9 billion sustainable lives possible by 2050?

Positive Thought Seven: Define Your Products' Contribution to the 9 Billion Challenge

Even once you know your product story; remember that it only applies to today.

Let's develop that story further. Answer the following question:

What is your products' contribution to helping create 9 billion quality and sustainable lifestyles by 2050?

Where are you making sustainable lifestyles more likely to happen? Where are you making them harder to happen because of your by-products or inefficiencies in your supply chain?

Remember those Halloween products? Does a plastic witch's hat make it easier for us to achieve 9 billion sustainable lifestyles, or harder?

Halloween supports manufacturing and retail jobs, and is a significant retail event, but does that balance with its contribution to 9 billion sustainable lives? When many of us were children in the 1950s and 60s, we made Halloween costumes and cakes with our parents. It was a two or three hour interaction: cutting up a cornflake packet to make a mask, which we then threw away at the end of the day. What Wal-Mart and others are making us do is go into Wal-Mart to buy Halloween costumes, sweets, baskets; all in sacks. Parents say "there you are kids, put that on!" And then we wonder where the disconnect between parents and their children comes from. Buying plastic Halloween masks made in China has an impact on our supply chains, on our planet, and on our relationships. Is this what we intend?

In the UK, outdoor heater sales dropped when retailers were challenged on the simple question: *"What is the point of outdoor heating?"* If it is too cold to sit outdoors, wear a jumper: that was the logic of the challenge. Don't tempt us with gas guzzling products to help stay outside for just a bit longer.

Many of us have seen a certain Coca Cola campaign. It shows a bottle of Coca Cola with the slogan "open happiness" – implying that happiness can be had by drinking a bottle of Coca Cola. Does that really make 9 billion sustainable lives more achievable? Or harder? Coca Cola, however, are also launching new brands (such as health drinks), and using these brands to encourage exercise – that has a very different and (many would argue) useful contribution.

Every product story should be aligned with making it easier for the world to deliver 9 billion sustainable lives, and with reducing, or even eliminating, elements that make it harder.

How do businesses do more? Think about this as a challenge, especially when market research shows that, while customers want a more sustainable lifestyle, they do not necessarily rush out and buy every eco-labelled product, preferring instead to stick to the brand and price points and short-term needs from the products they seek.

The answer is simple – you work *with* that preference rather than trying to change it. Customers do not seek out safe products, they expect them. Likewise, they expect their favourite brands and retailers to make these difficult decisions and judgements for them. Sustainability is less a customer choice and more a customer service – sustainable products are best delivered by 'choice editing'.

Positive Thought Eight: Edit, Rather than Inform, Consumer Choice

Many companies become nervous about sustainability because their customers are not asking for it, let alone demanding it.

Market research is ambiguous - exposing concern for the environment, but a reluctance to pay more or compromise quality. This is seen by some as justification for inaction. Such a conclusion is flawed, and needs to be challenged. It makes a false assumption of choice, and a second false assumption that sustainability will compromise price and quality. Short term, maybe. But if we agree that unsustainability is unsustainable, then companies should be preparing for it regardless of customer feedback.

Customers did not demand bar codes or pallets, but the supply chain thrives as a result of them – the same must be true for sustainability.

Customers are, however, fickle. They respect a brand that takes on these issues, especially one that does it without the price or quality compromise. Meanwhile, they are quick to look down on a brand that gets it wrong.

Most companies fear a child labour or sweat shop scandal in their supply chain or product story. They also would prefer (if not expect) that the brands they buy from be on top of these long term trends. The 'ask' of the customer is that this be achieved in a way that does not compromise their current lifestyles. This once again re-enforces a central point in this narrative: that sustainable development is about finding the means to deliver more and better quality, modern plasma TV lifestyles. That is, this is less about pure consumer choice, and more about embedding the right things into all the products and services they are offered.

Consumer choice, with or without eco-labels, will not be the major driver of change. Sustainability can help public relations and marketing, but it should not be the reason for doing it.

B&Q is a good example – their customers can only buy timber from well managed forests. I called this lack of choice between green and not so green *"choice editing"* in the "I Will if You Will" report I co-authored (see bibliography). Choice editing helps the price issue, because the volume helps reduce the price and inventory costs – it is cheaper for a retailer to offer one item than two.

How many people would not have bought their child the latest Harry Potter book because it was not printed on FSC paper? How many people only bought Harry Potter because it was printed on FSC paper? But Harry Potter was one of FSC's largest interventions at the time. It was the publisher who just decided to do it; an excellent example of choice editing

Choice editing is not confined to higher cost products. At Sainsbury's (a UK retailer), the cheapest toilet paper is FSC certified. It's a procurement standard. Even if you want to supply Sainsbury's with the lowest cost toilet paper they are prepared to buy, you will still have to have that toilet paper certified. Another example of "choice editing".

Positive Thought Nine: Use Sustainability to Challenge Your Business Model

Forty years ago, we worried about garbage. This led to the phrase, "reduce, reuse and recycle." Recycled paper is now a major component of newsprint. Recycled tyres find their way into roads, playgrounds, and many other products. Recycled building products are being used in restoration projects around the world.

New business models were created to solve the waste mountain. It continues – we have businesses producing energy from landfills. The City of Edmonton in Alberta, for example, has built a facility which is processing 100,000 tonnes of municipal solid waste into 36 million litres of biofuels annually, which will help reduce Alberta's carbon dioxide (CO_2) footprint by six million tonnes over the next 25 years. Again, this innovation was driven by the creation of new business models, not by what many call corporate social responsibility (CSR).

The CSR agenda tinkers with existing business models and, while that can be helpful, it would not have created the breakthroughs that led to the new waste management business models that exist today.

CSR is about meeting today's consumer expectations on social and environmental issues. Some, however, might argue that that's just good business. Some push CSR a bit further, saying it is about predicting and preparing for future consumer expectations. This is what B&Q did. It was thinking ahead of its time. It took 20 years to achieve certification for every timber product B&Q sells, but it would be a messy place today if it had done nothing.

Buying timber from well managed forests was, and still is, good CSR – but it also ensures that there will be enough timber to supply 9 billion quality lifestyles by 2050, let alone B&Q's own growth.

That supply chain challenge is what separates good CSR from corporate sustainability. Corporate sustainability starts with the capacity of the planet to meet those needs, NOT with the explicit demands of the customer. In many cases, they will be the same; but not in every case. CSR works within the constraints of the current business model, but sustainability challenges today's model, and forces business leaders to seek out new ones. If the business model is wrong, there will be no business case that works for sustainability.

In 2011, the CEO of Kingfisher, parent of B&Q, made the observation that the average power drill sold by his DIY stores (like B&Q) only does a total few minutes' work over its lifespan before being replaced by a newer model. The customer buys a drill because they need it to complete a specific job, drills a few holes, puts up their shelves, and puts the drill in their garage. Two years later, they have another job to do, so they go out and buy the latest model.

B&Q was selling a product at a very low price which does a few minutes' work before it is replaced. The demands on the planet's resources – e.g. impact of metal mining, transportation and manufacture – for these few minutes are considerable. Even if all the sources were ethical, the sheer amount of 'stuff' required and waste generated would be too much to supply 9 billion with drills in this 'few minute use' model. The CEO admitted that it was time to look at the idea of leasing the drill for the duration of the job, rather than selling it. He is looking at changing the current business model, which will never be justified in the interests of sustainability.

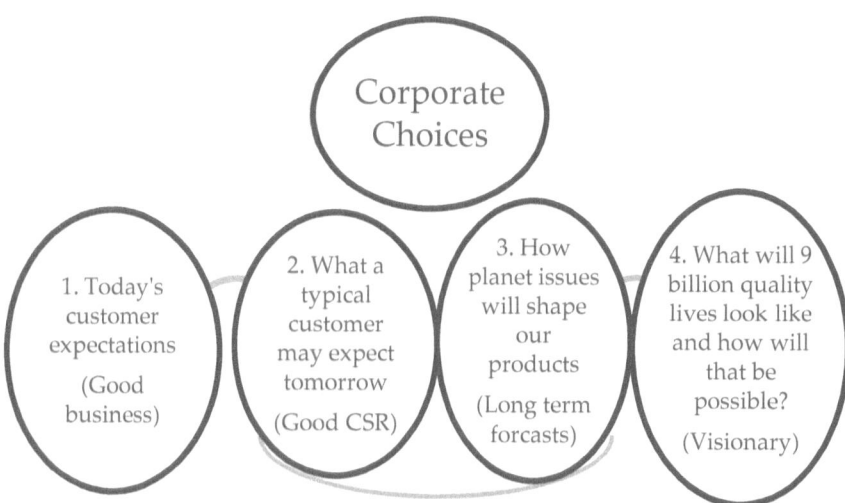

There is currently no business case, at least for the next fifteen years or so, to fly an aircraft by using fuel made in part from biofuel, or even recycled CO_2. But if you're interested in a long-term business model for sustainability, that is what the future of aviation looks like.

Richard Branson, whose airline *Virgin Atlantic* was the first commercial airline to test biofuel, has gone even further. Is there a business taking yesterday's carbon dioxide out of the air? Rather than sequestration during the production process, can we capture CO_2 (which has a great many beneficial uses) from the atmosphere? This is less mad than it sounds – he is applying the waste hierarchy to greenhouse gases. What we want is an economy where carbon goes around in natural processes, rather than burning 200 million year old fossil carbons, and putting them in the sky.

In 2007, Sir Richard Branson launched the Virgin Earth Challenge. A U.S. $25 million prize was offered to anyone who could demonstrate a commercially viable design which resulted in the net removal of anthropogenic, atmospheric greenhouse gases to the judges' satisfaction. Once an idea is proven as able to work, the challenge changes – to get it to work on a commercial and global scale; something Virgin companies have a lot of experience with.

Sustainability must harness true innovative capacity to undertake the needed development (since the research is there) to make this viable. Such interventions will not pass a business case-type thinking – they are completely new business models. It is not science fiction - the Earth Challenge received over 2600 applications, and in November 2011, the finalists were announced in Calgary, Alberta.

Virgin Atlantic, also in 2011, announced a strategic partnership with LanzaTech, a Swedish company with technology that can recycle methane and CO_2. They are using emissions from a steel mill to make jet fuel, so recycling CO_2 from thin air might one day be possible. Other companies are finding other uses for recycled CO_2; linking green houses to newsprint production; taking the CO_2 emitted in the pulping process and using it to grow tree seedlings to replant the forest. Five distribution vehicles operated by Arla Foods' distribution centre in Copenhagen are refrigerated by recycled CO_2, sourced from other companies' production. There are many more examples. Yes, we need to reduce emissions, but we also need to recycle and reuse those emissions into something useful.

Conclusion

The narrative of sustainable development between now and 2050 will experience a high degree of de-toxing. The emotions of blame, guilt, and judgment will be replaced with optimism, inspiration and direction.

We will stop telling people what they are doing wrong and instead highlight what they can do right.

Sustainable development will not be a moral choice, but a practical challenge; and one where every element of civil society will make a contribution. It's not about good or bad. It will be seen as a project that requires practical and coordinated thinking. Contradictions will be purged and will be replaced by a can-do, project focused, practical approach, free from judgment and ideology.

Maybe the simplest answer is that we should manage the planet's resources in the same way supermarkets manage their supply chains. Businesses maximize their ability to provide what their consumers want in such a way that it helps grow their business. A supermarket, for example, would never meet customer demands by cannibalizing the health of its finances or infrastructure. That basic management skill will be transferred to those with a say in how the larger natural resources of the planet will be managed.

In the 1900s and 2000s, procurement policy drove considerable change in natural resources management. In the 2020s and beyond, data about the economic value natural resources bring to national economies will result in more land use decisions being made by the nations who own those resources, in close collaboration with the markets. Public policy will have the data and incentives to make better long-term decisions. We can only do that through a shift from campaigns and criticism to conversation and collaboration.

The dream in my rethinking of corporate sustainability is a world where every company, every organisation in the world could answer this question:

> My product's positive and negative contribution towards helping the world achieve 9 billion sustainable lifestyles by 2050 is as follows....

It's subtle but it's very different from "You are bad because...."

And that's what I'm talking about: changing the narrative. While retailers currently contribute to a lot of the problems we are trying to solve, they do have some disciplines which are useful in providing the answers to that key question.

My experience, observation and insights suggest that this is a positive way forward – a way of rethinking our understanding of corporate social responsibility.

BIBLIOGRAPHY

Knight, AP, Mayo E (2006), *I will if you will*, Sustainable Consumption Roundtable, Sustainable Development Commission and National Consumer Council, London

Knight, AP (2009), *Sustainable Lifestyles*, Sustainable Development Commission, London